PERCUSSION G

The book was written using the Carl Orff approach.

Orff believed that each child should not be a passive listener, but an active co-creator. He/she must have the opportunity to act and dance to accompany a composition and improvise while listening to or learning to play music.

With this book, you can be your kids' Orrf music instructor, who encourages a child's natural sense of music, even if they have never played music before.

THIS BOOK CONSISTS OF 2 SECTIONS

1. The first, with the "3 Little Pigs" fairy tales, not only can you and your kids play using a percussion instrument musical set, but also with any other musical sounds you can come up with. You can easily change the musical instruments for adding different sounds or creating new activities when playing with your child. This game illustrates how any simple story or fairy tale can be accompanied by musical activity.

2. The second part has games to be played with a tambourine. These games develop phonetic listening and kids rhythmic skills, which are required for reading and writing. Be creative and use these rhythms for any other songs you may want to use.

THE THREE LITTLE PIGS, WITH MUSICAL SCORE

Onomatopoeia develops children's creative imagination, and introduces skills for playing percussion musical instruments. Children learn to adjust the volume and strength of sounds, enhance their listening skills, and develop their gross and fine motor skills. If several children are playing, they learn to wait their turn and develop patience. While reading the fairy tale, all music instruments should be easily accessible (i.e., lay out in front of or around the kids). For the first time, an adult should read the story and play the instrument by themself, with the kids only listening. Later, if the child is small, you can divide the instruments, giving kids only some of them for musical scoring. Later, the kids can play all the instruments, and even recite the whole fairy tale and score themselves. Encourage the kids if they suggest their own method of scoring or their own plot of the fairy tale.

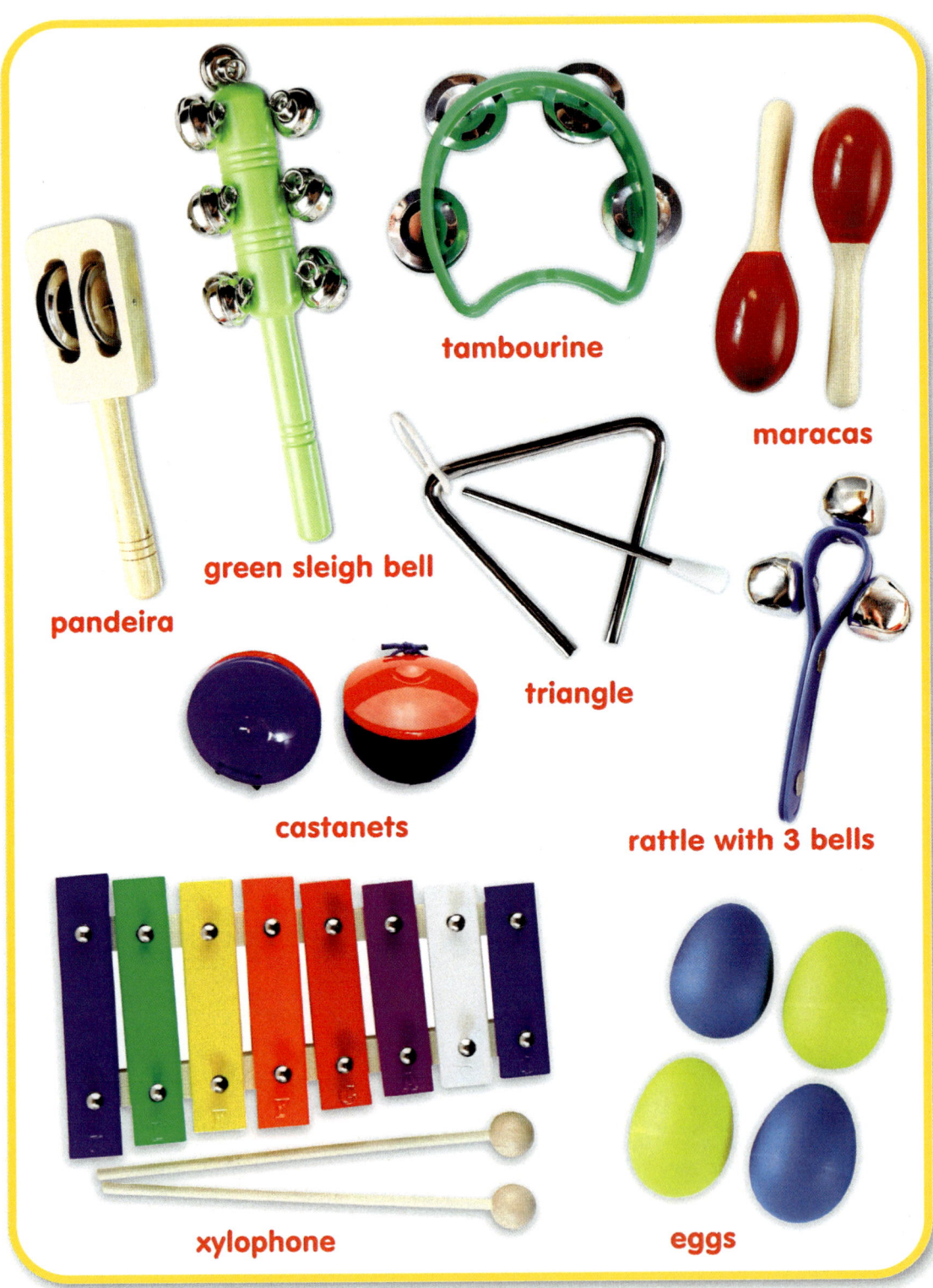

tambourine

maracas

green sleigh bell

pandeira

triangle

castanets

rattle with 3 bells

xylophone

eggs

Create sounds:

Slide the mallet along
all the notes of the xylophone

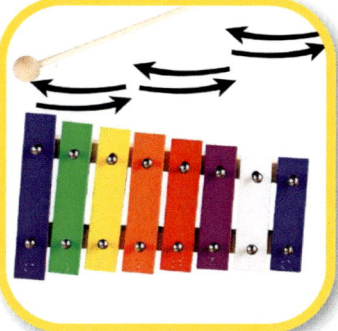

Slide the mallet back
and forth along 2-3 notes
on the xylophone

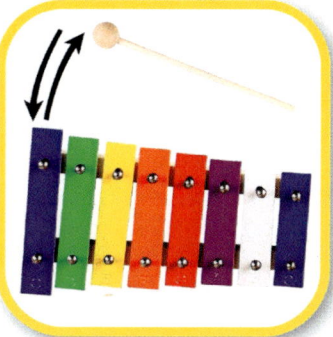

Hit note C several times

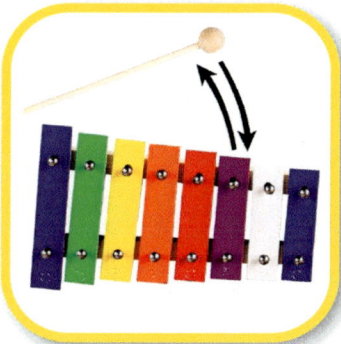

Hit note A several times

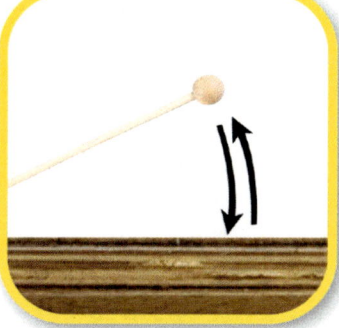

Knock the mallet
on table

Shake pandeira

Shake tambourine

Hit tambourine on table

Shake the eggs

Hit the triangle

Shake the rattle with 3 bells

Shake the green sleigh bell

Shake the maracas

Click the castanets

Rustle the polybag

Make growl sounds

Make howl sounds

Make blow sounds

THE THREE LITTLE PIGS

There once were 3 little pigs.

They were small and very merry *(pandeira shaking)*,

playing in their wonderful place by the river

(shaking tambourine).
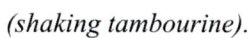

It was summer and they frolicked in the sun and had

a wonderful time running *(xylophone sound slowly from G to G)*,

swimming *(xylophone splashes)*

and playing in the sand *(shaking eggs)*.

One morning, they heard a knock on a tree *(castanets knocks)*.

They looked up and saw a woodpecker. The woodpecker asked them

where they were going to spend the winter because it was

getting colder. The carefree pigs hadn't thought about winter.

They continued to sing, *(shaking pandeira)*

and danced

(shaking tambourine)

and play together the rest of the day. *(3 bells rattle shaking)*

Several days later they heard a sleigh bell.

(green sleigh bell sound).

They looked up and saw a horse with a

cart passing by. The horse asked them

where they were going to stay over the

winter, which was upon them.

The happy-go-lucky piggies had

not made any plans yet.

It was only when it became colder, the rain began to come

very often *(beat 3 times note A on the xylophone)*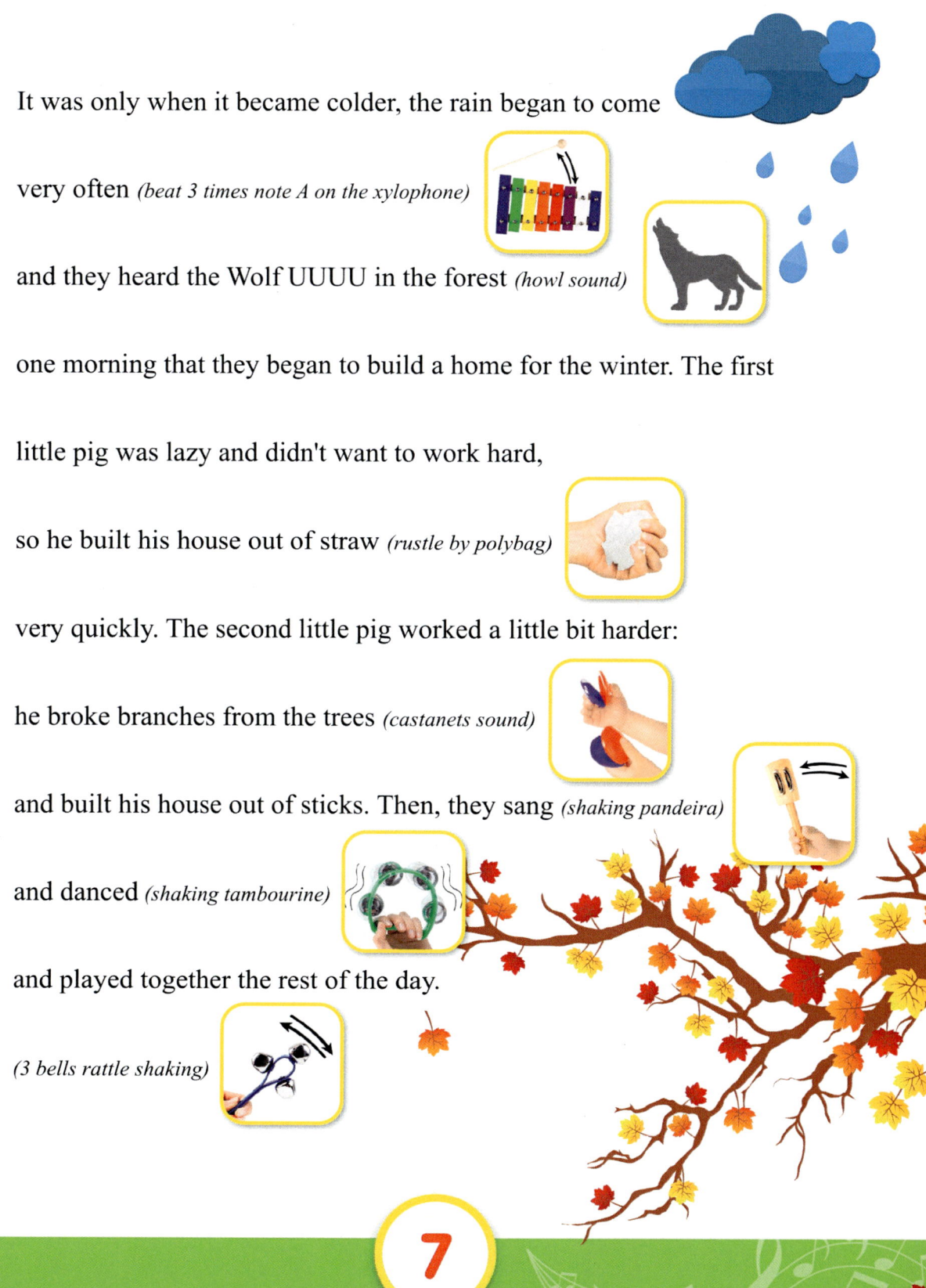

and they heard the Wolf UUUU in the forest *(howl sound)*

one morning that they began to build a home for the winter. The first

little pig was lazy and didn't want to work hard,

so he built his house out of straw *(rustle by polybag)*

very quickly. The second little pig worked a little bit harder:

he broke branches from the trees *(castanets sound)*

and built his house out of sticks. Then, they sang *(shaking pandeira)*

and danced *(shaking tambourine)*

and played together the rest of the day.

(3 bells rattle shaking)

The third little pig worked hard for several days.

He took some sand from the river *(maracas sounds)*

and stirred it with water *(eggs sounds)*
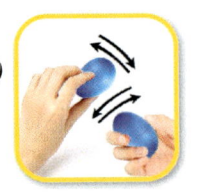

to make some bricks.

He built his house with the bricks, carefully

placing them one by one *(knock the mallet by the table)*.

It was a sturdy house complete with a fine fireplace and chimney.

It looked like it could withstand the strongest winds. He was very tired at

the end of the day, but very satisfied.

But the next day he sang *(shaking pandeira)*

and danced *(shaking tambourine)*

and played with

his brothers for the rest of the day.

(3 bells rattle shaking)

A week later, a wolf happened to pass by the lane where the three little

pigs lived; he saw the straw house, and he smelled the pig inside.

So he knocked on the door *(castanets sound)*,

rang in the doorbell *(triangle sound)*

and said:

RRRR *(growl sounds)*

«Little pig! Little pig! Let me in! Let me in!»

But the little pig saw the Wolf's big paws through the keyhole,

so he answered back:

«No! No! No! *(Hit small note C on the xylophone)*

Not by the hairs on my chinny chin chin!»

Then the Wolf showed his teeth and said:

«Then I'll huff and I'll puff and I'll blow your house

down». So he huffed and he puffed and he blew

the house down!

(green sleigh bell sound).

The Wolf opened his jaws very wide,

he snapped his teeth very loud *(castanets sound)*

and bit down as hard as he could *(knock hand on table)*,

but the first little pig escaped and

ran away very quickly *(xylophone C to C)*

to hide in the house of the second little pig and closed the door just near

the Wolf's nose

(hit tambourine on table).

The Wolf knocked on the door *(castanets sound)*,

rang the doorbell *(triangle sound)*

and said: RRRR

(growl sounds)

«Little pigs! Little pigs! Let me in! Let me in!»

But the little pigs saw the Wolf's pointy ears through the keyhole, so they

answered back: «No! No! No! *(hit small note C on the xylophone)*

Not by the hairs on our chinny chin chin!»

So the Wolf showed his teeth

and said: RRRR *(growl sounds)*

«Then I'll huff and I'll puff and I'll blow your house down».

So he huffed and he puffed and he blew

the house down! *(green sleigh bell sound)*.

The Wolf was greedy and he tried to catch both pigs at once,

but he was too greedy and got neither! His big

jaws clamped down on nothing *(castanets sound)*

but air and the two little pigs scrambled away as fast as

their little hooves would carry them. *(xylophone from C to C)*

The Wolf chased them down the lane and he almost caught them. But

they made it to the brick house and slammed the door closed just as the

Wolf's nose began to enter *(hit tambourine on table)*.

The three little pigs were very frightened. They

sat together and trembled with fear *(maracas sounds)*

because they knew the Wolf wanted to eat them.

And that was very, very true.

So he knocked on the door *(castanets sound)*,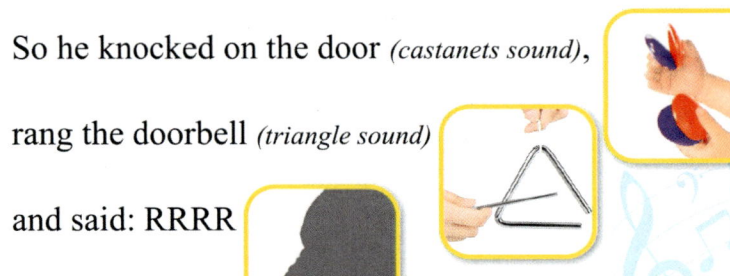

rang the doorbell *(triangle sound)*

and said: RRRR

(growl sounds)

«Little pigs! Little pigs! Let me in! Let me in!»

But the little pigs saw the Wolf's narrow eyes through the keyhole, so they

answered back: «No! No! No! *(hit note C on the xylophone)*

Not by the hairs on our chinny chin chin!»

So the Wolf showed his teeth *(castanets knock)*

and said: «Then I'll huff and I'll puff and I'll blow your house down». Well!

He huffed and he puffed *(blow)*.

He puffed and he huffed *(shaking maracas)*.

And he huffed, huffed *(rustling of packages)*,

and he puffed, puffed; *(green sleigh bell sound)*

but he could not blow the house down.

At last, he was so out of breath that he couldn't huff and he

couldn't puff anymore. So he stopped to rest and thought a bit.

Then he climbed on to the roof and even the roof shook *(shake eggs)*

and he jumped down the chimney. At that time, the piglets

were cooking soup. Water was boiling in a pot *(shake maracas)*

on the fire. Then, just as the Wolf was coming down the chimney,

the little piggy pulled off the lid, and plop! in *(hit triangle)*

fell the Wolf into the scalding water. Another little

pig opened the door at that time.

The Wolf howled, shook himself off and run out the door and

disappeared into the woods.

The little pig shut the door *(knock the mallet)*.

And then the 3 little pigs sang *(shaking pandeira)*

and danced *(shaking tambourine)*

and played together

for the rest of the day. *(3 bells rattle shaking)*.

They decided to live

together, never be lazy

and help each other.

13

PLAY
YOUR TAMBOURINE

14

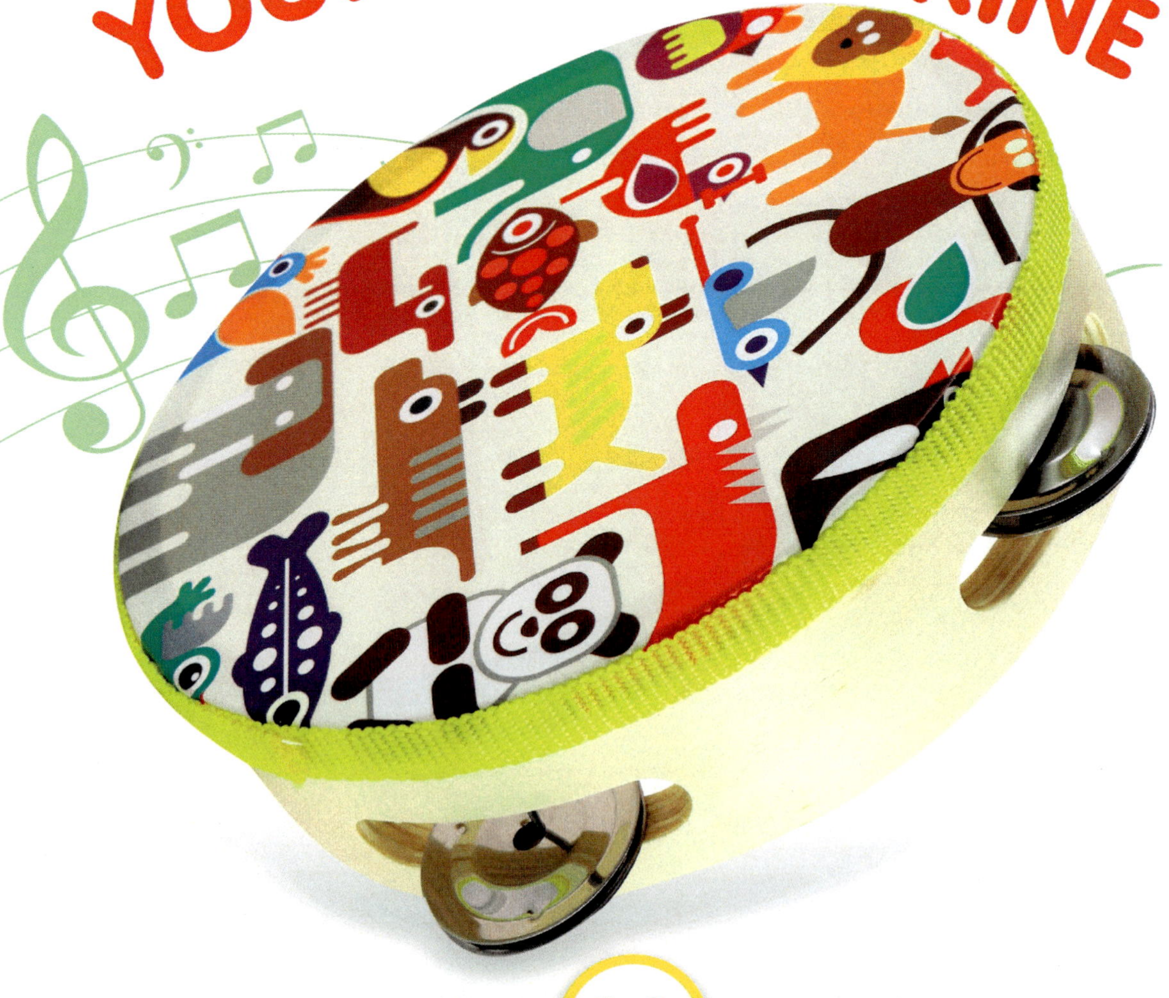

GAMES   WITH TAMBOURINE

Science has shown that there is a correlation between a sense of rhythm and a good grasp of grammar. Our tambourine helps develop both by developing phonetic listening in children. Below are several games that can be played with a tambourine for small kids that will teach them to maintain a beat and identify sounds.

DEVELOPS:

1. Phonetic listening
2. Rhythmic playing of children's songs
3. Rhythmic skills required for reading and writing

CONTENTS

1. Games with tambourine for Phonemic Awareness

2. Nursery rhymes with tambourine

3. Songs to play with Tambourine

Children will play the tambourine to the beat of the music. Popular kids' songs are written with an image of a tambourine at the word where they need to beat. You can accompany the child with xylophone, piano, voice, etc. This great exercise develops phonetic listening, a sense of rhythm and simple playing of a musical instrument.

Games with tambourine
for Phonemic Awareness
How many words?

Say each sentence and ask child to beat the tambourine on each word.

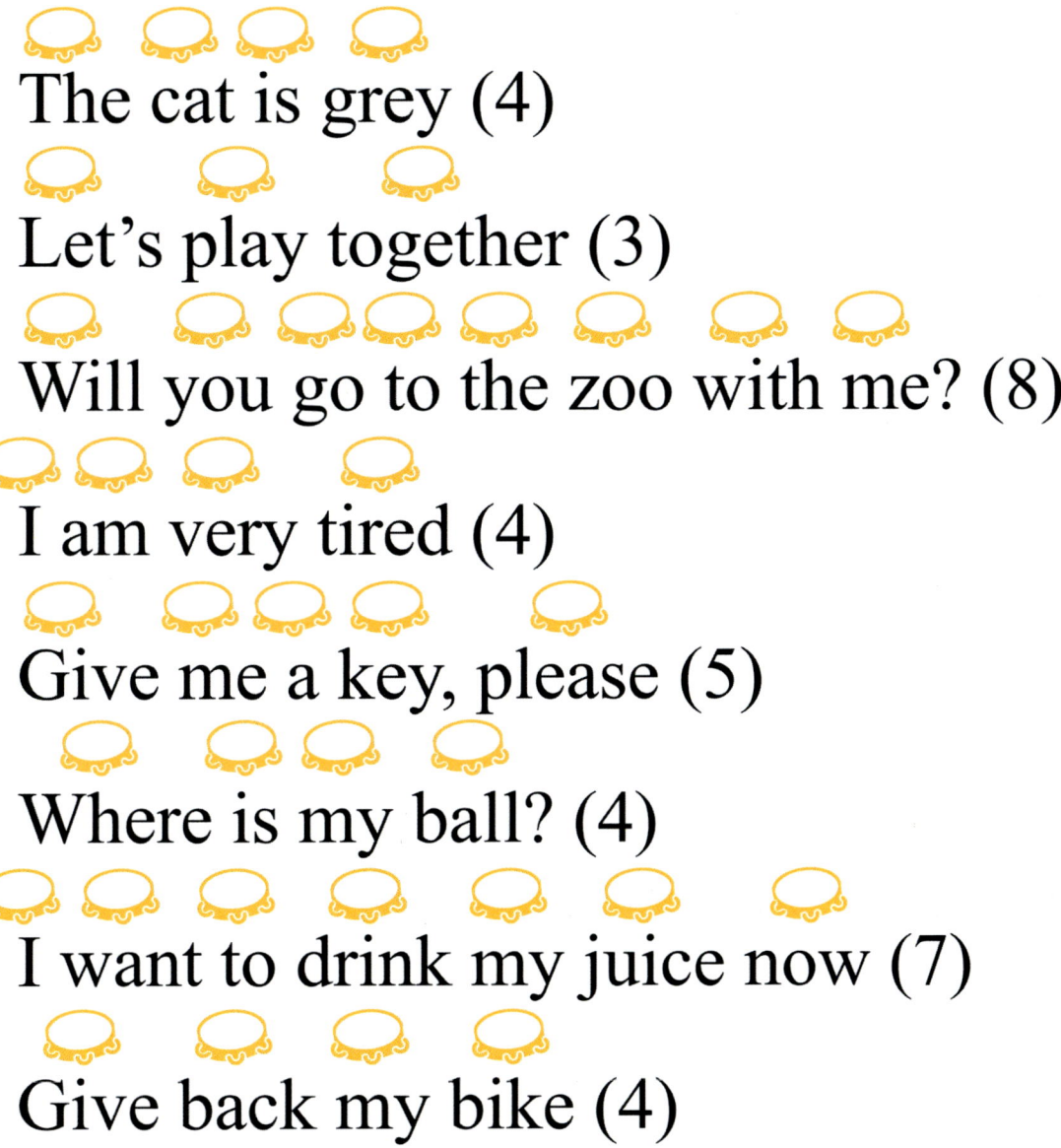

The cat is grey (4)

Let's play together (3)

Will you go to the zoo with me? (8)

I am very tired (4)

Give me a key, please (5)

Where is my ball? (4)

I want to drink my juice now (7)

Give back my bike (4)

Count syllables

Say each word and ask kid to repeat the word slowly and beat the tambourine according the syllables he/she hears (for each syllable)

Rain-coat (2)

Sat-ur-day (3)

Rasp-ber-ry (3)

Tam-bou-rine (3)

Bear (1)

Lake (1)

Fish (1)

Bell (1)

Rain-bow (2)

Catch the sound

Ask kids to find the sound (for example L) L in the words and beat the tambourine for each L

…. To find sound L

Sock

Plain

Red

Lake

Cat

Train

Lock

Cake

Light

Plate

…. To find sound B

Dark

Nose

Dog

Bird

Step

Bell

Steel

Battle

Plan

…. To find sound P

Gate

Leg

Man

Potato

Put

Route

Top

Bun

Print

Catch the word

Create some imagined words and read kids a list of words where the "fake" words are mixed in with the real words.

For example

bed

maf

scarf

saf

talk

chalk

plim

The child must beat the tambourine if he/she hears the "pretend" word.

Nursery rhymes with tambourine

Clapping Nursery rhymes or any Rhythmic circle lyrics are a great method for rhythm development.
Read the rhymes with children and beat the tambourine for each accented word in a line or for each repeated word in a rhyme.

Miss Mary Mack, Mack, Mack

Miss Mary Mack, Mack, Mack

All dressed in black, black, black

With silver buttons, buttons, buttons

All down her back, back, back.

She asked her mother, mother, mother

for fifty cents, cents, cents

To see the hippos, hippos, hippos

Jump the fence, fence, fence.

They jumped so high, high, high

they reached the sky, sky, sky

And didn't come back, back, back

Till the 4th of July, 'ly, 'ly!

She asked her mother, mother, mother

For 5 cents more, more, more

To see the hippos, hippos, hippos

Jump over the door, door, door.

They jumped so low, low, low

They stubbed their toe, toe, toe

And that was the end, end, end,

Of the hippo show, show, show!

Pat-a-cake

Pat-a-cake, pat-a-cake, baker's man.

Bake me a cake as fast as you can

Pat it, and prick it, and mark it with a "B"

And put it in the oven for baby and me!

Miss Polly had a dolly

Miss Polly had a dolly who was sick, sick, sick.

So she phoned for the doctor to be quick, quick, quick.

The doctor came with his bag and his hat

And he knocked at the door with a rat-a-tat-tat.

He looked at the dolly and he shook his head

And he said "Miss Polly, put her straight to bed!"

He wrote on a paper for a pill, pill, pill

"I'll be back in the morning, yes

I will, will, will."

Lemonade

Lemonade,

Lemonade,

crunchy ice,

Sip it once.

Sip it twice.

Lemonade,

Crunchy Ice,

Made it once.

Made it twice.

Turn around,

Touch the ground,

Kick your boyfriend out of town! *(shaking the tambourine)*

Freeze!

To market, to market

To market, to market, to buy a fat pig,

Home again, home again, jiggety-jig.

To market, to market, to buy a fat hog,

Home again, home again, jiggety-jog.

To market, to market, to buy a plum bun,

Home again, home again, market is done

Songs to play with Tambourine

Hot Cross Buns

Hot Cross Buns,

Hot Cross Buns,

One a penny,

two a penny,

Hot Cross Buns

Are you sleeping?

Are you sleeping, are you sleeping?

Brother John, Brother John?

Morning bells are ringing,

morning bells are ringing

Ding ding dong, ding ding dong.

Mary Had
A Little Lamb

Mary had a little lamb

Little lamb, little lamb

Mary had a little lamb

Its fleece was white as snow

The Wheels On The Bus

The wheels on the bus go round and round.

Round and round.Round and round.

The wheels on the bus go round and round.

Round and round.

Twinkle, Twinkle Little Star

Twinkle, twinkle, little star,

How I wonder what you are.

Up above the world so high,

Like a diamond in the sky.

Old MacDonald Had A Farm

Old McDonald had a farm. E-I-E-I-O.

And on that farm he had a cow.

E-I-E-I-O.

With a moo moo here.

With a moo moo there.

Here a moo.

There a moo.

Everywhere a moo moo.

Old McDonald had a farm. E-I-E-I-O.

Do You Know
The Muffin Man?

Oh, do you know the muf-fin man,

The muf-fin man, the muf-fin man.

Oh, do you know the muf-fin man.

That lives on Drury Lane?

London Bridge is Falling Down

London Bridge is falling down,

Falling down, falling down.

London Bridge is falling down,

My fair lady.

Jingle bells

Jingle bells, jingle bells,

jingle all the way

Oh, what fun it is to ride

in a one horse open sleigh

Jingle bells, jingle bells,

jingle all the way

Oh, what fun it is to ride

in a one horse open sleigh

We wish you a Merry Christmas

We wish you a Merry Christmas

We wish you a Merry Christmas

We wish you a Merry Christmas

And a Happy New Year

Happy Birthday

Happy birthday to you

Happy birthday to you

Happy birthday dear Mary

Happy birthday to you

Manufactured by Amazon.ca
Bolton, ON